Y0-CBT-978

Loyal For Life

How to Take Unhappy Customers From

Hell to Heaven in 60 Seconds or Less

JOHN TSCHOHL

Best Sellers Publishing
9201 East Bloomington Freeway
Minneapolis, Minnesota 55420,
USA.
Phone: 952-888-7672
Fax: 952-884-8901
E-mail:
bsp@bestsellerspublishing.com
www.bestsellerspublishing.com

Library of Congress Cataloging-in-
Publication Data

Tschohl, John
    Loyal for Life by John Tschohl
John Tschohl
      p. cm.
    Includes index.
    ISBN 0-9636268

    1. Customer service. III. Title
    HF54 15.5T83
      658.8'12---dc2o   95-080722
                      CIP

Loyal for Life reminds us that we are our brand, and *every* customer experience either strengthens or weakens the brand. Bravo John.

Vernon W. Hill II, Chairman of the Board
     President
     Commerce Bank

Loyal for Life is another contribution to the service industry in the world made by my friend and partner John Tschohl, "guru of customer service". This very book will surely make another impact, as his previous four books have done, on the service sector in China. I strongly recommend this book to professionals and practitioners in the service sector.

Gu Jiadong, CEO
Shanghai Foreign Service Co. Ltd.

John has once again focused on service, loyalty and service recovery as the key ingredients for outstanding profitable and maintainable growth; he sights many examples in a fast paced readable work.

Robert Hunter, D.M.D.
CEO of DentaQuest Ventures, Inc.

Tschohl always offers a practical spin on customer service and finds new ways to make us think about the customer.

Don Stricklin, President and CEO
Texas United Bancshares, Inc

Table of Contents

SERVICE RECOVERY BOOK

I have been very fortunate to have a great wife and family who have tolerated my obsession with customer service for some three decades now. My wife Pat, daughter Christina, and son Matthew have made life worth living. They also have caught on to the service strategy message and have become savvy consumers who demand exceptional customer service.

My mother, who died a few years ago at 102 years of age, was responsible for much of my success. She inspired me and believed in me, and I miss her. I also miss Hazel Brown, my administrative assistant, who retired last year after 29 years of working with me at the Service Quality Institute.

This book never would have been written without Vicki Stavig, my writer and publicist. I thank her for her help in getting my customer service message out there.

Preface

I've been preaching the importance of customer service for some 25 years now. I recognized early on that it would become an increasingly important factor in whether or not a company would succeed. And yet it is missing in most companies throughout the world.

So it was that I founded the Service Quality Institute 33 years ago, in 1972, and have since developed and presented 40 customer service training programs to organizations throughout the world.

While customer service is critical to the success of any organization, I also recognize that even the Amazon.coms of the world occasionally make a mistake. How organizations and their employees

Most executives have no idea what service recovery is.

deal with those mistakes separates the customer service leaders from the rest of the pack.

I've also come to realize that most executives have no idea what service recovery is. And if they don't know what it is, they certainly can't expect their employees to practice it.

So it is that I am writing this book, a primer in essence, on service recovery. Within these pages I define service recovery, tell you how to implement it, identify service recovery leaders, and give you some ideas on how in 60 seconds or less you can transform an angry customer into a happy—and loyal—customer who will sing your praises to anyone who will listen.

1 What is Service Recovery?

Simply put, service recovery is putting a smile on a customer's face after you've screwed up. It's solving a customer's problem or complaint and sending him out the door feeling as if he's just done business with the greatest company on earth. And it's doing so in 60 seconds or less.

Unfortunately, few executives and managers understand service recovery—and, if they don't understand it, it's a given that their employees don't either. It's critical for the success of any organization that everyone, from the CEO to the frontline employee, understands and practices service recovery. If they don't, customers not only will defect, they will take potential customers with them as they

Service recovery is the step that should follow a mistake.

spread the word about their dissatisfaction with your organization.

Service recovery is more advanced and significantly more powerful than simply saying you're sorry. It's a tool that builds customer loyalty, that brings a customer back from the brink of defection.

Service recovery is the step that should follow a mistake. You should apologize, take responsibility for the error or the inconvenience, and give the customer something of value as compensation. Taking those steps creates an environment where the customer will be so satisfied that she will tell five to 10 others about what you did for her.

To simply say you're sorry is nice, but it's not very powerful. To give the customer $5 or a minor gift has no real impact or ability to stop that customer from defecting. What you give to that customer as compensation must have value in her eyes. It has to be something so powerful that she not only will continue to patronize your business but she will tell everyone she knows about the wonderful service you provided to her.

While that compensation won't cost you much, it will be worth a million dollars in word-of-mouth advertising. A bookstore employee, for example, should have the authority to say, "I am so sorry for the error, Mr. Song. It is our fault and, as a way of apologizing, I'd like to give you a free book."

Now, you know that Mr. Song is going to accept that apology—and the book—and will happily tell his family, friends, and coworkers about the wonderful service he received at that bookstore. Nothing is as powerful as a personal recommendation from a satisfied customer.

While skiing with a friend in Vail, the chair lift stopped. Three times during the next hour, members of the ski patrol came by to update us on the situation. The final time they told us there was a gift waiting for us at the top of the mountain. When we got there, we

Nothing is as powerful as a personal recommendation from a satisfied customer

were greeted by three Vail employees, who apologized for inconveniencing us and who gave us two lift tickets along with a ticket for a free drink.

For the rest of that day and the next, we bragged to everyone we shared a chair lift with about what had happened and what we had been given. This is what service recovery is all about. The skiers who had been stranded on the chair lift at Vail were overly happy and spread the word to anyone who would listen about the wonderful treatment they had received. That was powerful word-of-mouth advertising.

Vail Resorts is ranked one of the leading resort operators in North America by the readers of Ski magazine. I believe it also has the best customer service in the world. I talked with Clyde Wiessner, Director of Lifts at Vail, about its service recovery policies. "We do what we think is appropriate for the situation at hand. We have a system in place where we empower employees to take care of our customers" he said. It was

Service Recovery is powerful word of mouth advertising.

Every company has something of value it can give to a customer who has experienced a problem.

no accident, he added, that the Guest Service and Ski Patrol had greeted us as we came off the chair lift at the top of the mountain or that they had coupons for free lift tickets and drinks ready for us.

Every company has something of value it can give to a customer who has experienced a problem. What do you manufacture, sell, or provide as a service that doesn't cost you a lot but that has value in the eyes of your customers and will send them away with smiles on their faces?

In order for service recovery to work, it must be implemented by frontline employees who have more contact with customers than anyone else in the company. Those employees must be trained in the art of customer service and empowered to make decisions that will result in satisfied and loyal customers. They should not need the approval of a supervisor or manager to do so. Policies and procedures that support and reinforce service recovery also must be in place.

It is helpful, during service recovery training, to have employees role play. Have them practice apologizing to the customer and adding value by giving the customer a gift, ideally a product or service. Spending money to keep a current customer is much less expensive than advertising and marketing to get new customers. Service recovery is the glue that cements customers to your business. The Service Quality Institute in Minneapolis, Minnesota, has created a one-session program to train employees in the art of service recovery.

Most employees will lie when they make a mistake. Few are comfortable taking responsibility for a problem that either they or the company created. It's important, therefore, that employees are trained in service recovery and empowered to compensate the customer. They also must have enough self-confidence and self-esteem to accept responsibility for the problem—and probably to endure some initial anger from the customer—and then apologize

Service Recovery is the glue that cements customers to your business.

The higher up a problem escalates, the higher the cost of dealing with it.

sincerely and give the customer something that will soothe his savage soul.

If one of your goals is to reduce the number of customer complaints directed at your organization, service recovery is the most powerful weapon in your arsenal. An effective service recovery plan not only will reduce complaints, it will result in positive responses from customers.

When frontline employees practice service recovery, it keeps the cost of handling the customer's problem to a minimum. The higher up a problem escalates, the higher the cost of dealing with it. The problem is that very few customers actually will complain when they have a problem with your company. Most of them will simply defect. Your cost per defecting customer might range from $1,000 to $50,000, depending on the lifetime value of that customer. The impact of a frontline employee mastering service recovery has a much higher value and impact than if an executive handles the problem. It costs the company less and it has a more powerful and immediate impact on the customer.

Many large companies have consumer affairs departments that will send a free product or a coupon for a free product to customers who complain. General Mills is one of them. While checking in for a flight recently, Homeland Security representatives confiscated from my luggage gravy flour made by General Mills because they identified it as having a risky chemical. When I sent General Mills a copy of my complaint letter to Homeland Security, the company sent me two free coupons for Wondra flour. That was service recovery.

Service recovery will put you and your organization ahead of the competition. It will prevent customer defection, which will increase your sales and profits. It also will prevent employee defection. When employees are trained in customer service and are empowered to make decisions that will satisfy their customers, they are happier in their jobs.

With service recovery, your customers—and your employees— wouldn't dream of leaving you.

Service Recovery will put you and your organization ahead of the competition.

Tips for Providing Quality Service Recovery

- **Act Quickly**
- **Take Responsibility**
- **Be Empowered**
- **Compensate**

Act quickly

The employee at the point of contact best implements service recovery.

Avoid moving problems and complaints up the chain of command.

Take Responsibility

- Take responsibility no matter who is at fault.
- Sincerely apologize.
- Don't place blame.
- Thank the customer for pointing out the problem.

DON'T make excuses or lie to cover a mistake.

DON'T point out a customer's misunderstanding.

DON'T pass the blame off to another employee or the organization.

Be Empowered

- Gives those who work with customers the authority to do whatever it takes to ensure customer loyalty.
- Empowerment is the backbone of service recovery.
- Tells customers that you will put them first.

Empowerment constrained by policy is really **NO** empowerment.

Compensate

Give the customer something of value.

Every organization has something of value it can give to a customer who has experienced a problem.

What does your organization manufacture, sell, or provide as a service that costs less than the value it has in the eyes of your customers?

Service recovery can turn angry customers into customers who will be *Loyal for Life*-all in just 60 seconds or less.

10 NOTES

2 From Hell to Heaven

Show me a company that has never made a mistake in serving a customer, and I'll show you a company that is in deep denial. Every company—no matter how excellent its products or employees—occasionally makes a mistake. How those companies and their employees respond to those mistakes, however, is what separates successful, customer-service driven organizations from the rest of the pack.

Companies that are committed to service recovery know they can win customers for life by solving their customers' problems. They go beyond the call of duty to make sure their customers are happy—with their products and their service. If it is within

Keeping the business of current customers is a lot cheaper than trying to replace those customers.

their ability to solve a customer's problem, they will move heaven and earth to do so. In the process they will take those customers from hell to heaven in 60 seconds or less.

Research shows that only one out of 26 people complain when they have a problem with a company. Those who do often are faced with a front-line employee who is seldom trained, rarely empowered, and often couldn't care less about that customer's complaint. Sixty-three percent of customers who have a problem that involves a purchase of less than $5 won't do business with that company again. Ninety-one percent won't do business with the company again if their problem involves a purchase of more than $100. That's pretty serious.

The purpose of service recovery is to prevent customer defections, to have customers who are loyal for life. If you solve your customers' problems and resolve their complaints, they will stay with you. When customers complain, they are giving you the opportunity to keep their business. And keeping the business of current customers is a lot cheaper than trying to replace those customers.

Look at it this way: Solving a customer's problem and giving him something worth $50—a gift certificate for dinner for two, for example—is much more effective than attempting to court a new customer through $50 worth of advertising. In fact, if you walked into a newspaper or TV office and said you wanted to place an ad for $50, you'd probably be laughed right out the door.

Service recovery—solving a customer's problem and sending him away singing your praises—creates word-of-mouth advertising that is 10 times more powerful than advertising and 20 times cheaper. It also requires less work to solve a customer's problem immediately than to let it escalate to the point where

Service Recovery is 10 times more powerful than advertising — and 20 times cheaper.

it comes to the attention of the company's CEO or worse, the government agency that regulates your industry.

All it will take is 60 seconds or less.

With service recovery, you will turn an angry customer, who will bad mouth your company to anyone and everyone who will listen, into a loyal customer who will spread the word about your wonderful service and who will return to you time and time again. Your employees will have peace of mind, morale will be higher, and employee turnover will be lower. You'll have positive word-of-mouth advertising, and you'll have customers for life. And, all it will take is 60 seconds or less.

To customers, you **ARE** the organization.

You must provide service and answer questions that help customers make informed decisions.

You must deliver products and services in a timely manner.

You must resolve customer complaints.

3 | Service Strategy

Service leaders focus on keeping customers. They value their customers, because they know how critical loyal customers are to their success.

Service leaders know they are in the service business —not in the banking, restaurant, hotel, computer, airline, telecommunications, or health care business. They spend time and money training their employees in the art of customer service in order to provide the most exceptional service possible to keep their current customers and attract new ones.

The major reason most companies get failing grades in customer service is that

Most companies don't understand the financial impact and power of a service strategy.

they don't understand the financial impact and power of a service strategy. As a result, they spend virtually all of their marketing money trying to lure new customers. What they don't realize is that it is much less expensive—and much more effective—to spend that money to provide the type of service that will keep their current customers from defecting.

Service leaders—like Amazon, Dell, Vail Resorts, Delta Dental, Southwest Airlines, General Electric, Commerce Bank, and Land's End—have mastered six critical elements that drive their service strategy.

1. They drive superior customer service strategically. That means the CEO walks the talk and all levels of management reinforce the importance of customer service.
2. They make sure their policies, procedures, and systems are customer-friendly. That could range from the hours their businesses are open to the rules governing customer payments.

Service leaders eliminate policies and procedures that get in the way of providing superior service.

3. They hire good people and treat them well. Service leaders spend 30 to 50 percent of their time selecting, coaching, and managing people. On average, they hire 1 out of every 50 applicants, much more stringent than the 1 out of every 2 applicants their competitors sign on. Unlike many organizations that spend more money on maintenance of their copy machines than they do in caring for their employees, service leaders place great value on their employees.

4. They empower their employees. They give them the authority to bend and break the rules, to use their common sense, to take care of the customer. Empowerment is the backbone of service recovery. If the frontline employee doesn't have the authority to do whatever is

Empowerment is the backbone of service recovery.

necessary to satisfy the customer, service recovery does not exist.

5. They train every employee in the art of service, using new materials at least every six months. Too many companies train their employees once—right after they're hired—and expect them to be customer-service stars for the rest of their lives. Just as companies like Coca Cola spend millions of dollars every day on advertising and know the importance of changing their commercials and print ads constantly in order to capture audience interest, service leaders know the importance of changing their training programs at least every six months to ensure employees will be interested and, therefore, involved. Every employee, without exception, must be trained.

6. They know the financial impact superior customer service has on their sales and profits. They understand the importance of word-of-mouth advertising in

Every employee, without exception, must be trained.

Every company has something of value it can give to a customer who has experienced a problem.

growing the company's image—and revenues—and how service recovery can bolster that advertising.

Let me give you some examples of how these service leaders handle service recovery and, in the process, are wildly successful.

DentaQuest, based in Boston, Massachusetts, asks its customers what they want—then gives it to them. "We continually survey customers to find what guarantees are important to them," says Fay Donahue, president of the company, which is one of the country's largest third-party administrator of commercial dental insurance. "The key drivers are our customers. They want ID cards, claims to be paid, and answers to their questions."

DentaQuest administers dental benefits programs for employers, unions, and associations in 20 states, with 2.1 million members. It processes 3.9 million claims per year with 99.6 financial accuracy, answers more than 1 million customer calls each year with a 95 percent access rate, and processes more than 500,000 enrollment forms annually with an accuracy of more than 99 percent. The company has a reputation for excellence that is unsurpassed. In fact, in June 2003 it eared the prestigious Massachusetts Performance Excellence Award, which is modeled after the Malcolm Baldrige National Quality Award.

The folks at DentaQuest don't merely tell customers they will give them what they want; they put it in writing. The company's Guarantee of Superior Service not only is unique in the industry, it is unique, period. What I find amazing is that none of DentaQuest's competitors has copied, or even attempted to copy, that guarantee.

Essentially, what the guarantee does is put the company's money where its mouth is. For example, if the company does not provide a complete and accurate identification card for each subscriber within 15 calendar days, it

None of DentaQuest's competitors has copied, or even attempted to copy, the company's guarantee.

"It costs much more to get an account than to retain an account," says Denta Quest's Fay Donahue.

will pay the group $25 per identification card. Another service guarantee states that the company will resolve a customer's question immediately by phone or guarantee the customer an initial update within one business day and continuous follow-up through to resolution. If it does not do so, it will pay the group $50 per occurrence. Other service guarantees focus on processing, conversion, billing, management reports, and savings.

"It costs much more to get an account than to retain an account," says Donahue. "We want the customer to have that feeling that it's going to work. They want to know that, if they buy this product from you, they can be assured it will work, that they won't have employees coming into their office complaining. The second thing is the internal controls it puts on us. We know if we're not doing a good job. We can fix processes so it won't happen again. We're at 99.9 percent processing accuracy; that's why we can offer a guarantee."

SUPERIOR SERVICE GUARANTEE

DentaQuest is committed to providing the highest level of service to all our customers. That's why we have developed one of the industry's most comprehensive service guarantees. Our Superior Service Guarantee promises quality customer service in writing, and is backed by a comprehensive refund policy.

1.   THE GUARANTEE
   Quick Processing of Claims

During the course of a policy year, 90% of the group's claims will be processed accurately within 15 business days upon receipt of completed claims forms.

The Refund: the Administrative fee charged for the group's last month of service.

2   THE GUARANTEE
   No-Hassle Customer Relations

DentaQuest will either immediately resolve your question over the phone or guarantee you an initial update within one business day and continuous follow-up to resolution.

The Refund: $50 paid to the group per occurrence.

3.   T HE GUARANTEE
   Accurate and Quick Turnaround of ID Cards

A complete and accurate identification card for each subscriber will be mailed to the group or to subscribers' home within 15 business days of receipt of the completed enrollment application.

The Refund: $25 paid to the group per subscriber ID card.

4.   THE GUARANTEE
   Management Reports

At the request of the groups with more than 50 employees, three standard reports (one claims report and two utilization reports) will be mailed to each group within 15 business days following the end of each quarter.

The Refund: $50 per late package paid to the group.

DentaQuest's Superior Service Guarantee offers clients peace of mind that nothing will go wrong.

DentaQuest's Superior Service Guarantee offers clients peace of mind that nothing will go wrong. The goal is to help its brokers get and retain accounts. The company recognizes that its 8 million clients want speed and accuracy when it comes to claims, enrollment, and response to problems. The company's service is so superior that, during 2004, it made only 13 payouts.

DentaQuest's Superior Service Guarantee is so good that we're reprinting it here. I suggest that you study it carefully and then identify guarantees you can offer that would set you up as an example of a service recovery leader.

HomeBanc Mortgage Corporation, which is headquartered in Atlanta, Georgia, has made customer service and service recovery a major focus. That might be why the company has grown to become one of the largest independent mortgage lenders in the Southeast.

"Our vision is to become America's Most Admired Company," says James Lutz, director of service quality, adding that HomeBanc currently is ranked 20 on FORTUNE magazine's list of the '100 Best Companies to Work For.' "We know that the only way to achieve the vision is by holding fast to our mantra that the only sustainable advantage in business is world-class service. We don't just preach service, we live it on a daily basis."

As an example of that service, HomeBanc has a Customer Service Guarantee, one that Lutz says is, to his knowledge, the "only truly unconditional guarantee in the mortgage banking industry. If for any reason a customer is unhappy with their loan transaction experience, we will gladly refund their application fee [typically $375]. The only thing we ask for is feedback on how we can improve moving forward." The guarantee program was instituted in late 1999 and, says Lutz, during the first 11 months of 2003, fewer than five customers per 1,000, or .42 percent, chose to redeem

"We don't just preach service, we live it on a daily basis," says James Lutz of HomeBanc Mortgage Corporation.

When Service Recovery becomes a way of life, customers are loyal for life.

their guarantees. "All 1,200-plus associates are empowered to invoke on behalf of a less than satisfied customer," he adds.

The company also established the Ron Hicks Customer Service Award, which recognizes on a monthly basis outstanding acts of service within the company. "We make heroes out of those who serve our customers in an extraordinary way," Lutz says. "Each of the monthly winners is called on stage during our annual meeting and gets to spin a prize wheel for a chance to win. One person will walk away with $25,000, another will receive $10,000, and a third will win $5,000. The remaining nine associates on stage receive $1,000 each."

Service leaders like DentaQuest and HomeBanc know that service and service recovery is key to their success. For them, a service strategy becomes a way of life and their customers are loyal for life. If you want to set your company apart from your competitors, you would do well to do likewise.

4

Word-of-Mouth Advertising

Every company has hundreds of choices on how it can spend its advertising dollars. If your financial resources for advertising and marketing are unlimited, this book and the service recovery concept probably isn't relevant, or necessary.

But, if you want to grow your business rapidly and cost-effectively, word-of-mouth advertising will be your cheapest—and most effective—tool. And, more often than not, that advertising will be supplied by customers who at one time had a problem with your company but who were on the receiving end of service recovery that was so fantastic that they told everyone they know about you.

Service Recovery puts the wow! into service.

Service recovery puts the wow! into service and generates word-of-mouth advertising you couldn't buy if you wanted to. Service that is merely OK, or even good, will not generate word-of-mouth advertising. You must provide awesome, incredible service.

Many companies spend millions of dollars creating loyalty programs geared to getting customers to return to them time and time again. Unfortunately, those same companies fail to train their employees in the art of service and service recovery, which is more powerful and less expensive than any advertising or loyalty program you could invest in.

Service leaders know they can cut their marketing and advertising budgets by providing exceptional service, which occasionally can even garner some favorable publicity in the media.

Whenever you see an ad or a commercial for a company that is touting its customer service, watch your wallet. Ad agencies love to create media campaigns that feature smiling employees and that use all the buzz words. But I've found that, if they have to advertise it, they really don't have it.

People trust their friends more than they trust any advertising. They look to their friends to recommend companies they should patronize, from caterers to chiropractors. They even trust people they don't know more than they trust advertising. How many times have you checked into a hotel and asked one of the employees to recommend a good restaurant? You ask that person, because you believe he or she has eaten at many of the local restaurants and can give you an honest recommendation based on personal experience. That is powerful word-of-mouth advertising that draws new customers.

There is a great little restaurant in Sydney, Australia, called The Little Snail. The service and the food are superior. During a one-week period, I ate there

People trust their friends more than they trust any advertising.

three times. Nine months later, when I returned to Sydney, The Little Snail was the first restaurant I went to.

Most companies—no matter what products or services they are selling—think that, if you are dissatisfied with their service, you simply will never return. They are right, but you also will tell just about anyone who will listen about the bad experience you had with that company. So that company not only will lose you as a customer, it will lose all those potential customers, those people who heard about its poor service.

Research shows that a dissatisfied customer will tell at least five people about his or her bad experience with a company. On the other hand, people who have experienced superior service and had their complaints or problems addressed quickly and to their satisfaction will spread the word to countless people about your wonderful company and employees.

Superior service, supported by service recovery, will generate positive word-of-

Superior service, supported by Service Recovery, will generate positive word-of-mouth advertising, increase your customer loyalty, bring in new customers, and send your sales and profits soaring.

Word-of-mouth advertising is priceless.

mouth advertising, increase your customer loyalty, bring in new customers, and send your sales and profits soaring. If you doubt that, look at Amazon.com. In 1995, its first year in business, the company had sales of $511,000. Thanks to its exceptional service, by the end of 2004, Amazon.com had $6.9 billion in sales.

If you want similar results, provide superior service and practice service recovery. The word-of-mouth advertising it generates is priceless.

5 | Training is Critical

Your goal, no matter what business you're in, should be to have overly happy customers. The only way to realize that goal is to empower everyone at every level in your company to do whatever is necessary to satisfy the customer. That includes modifying policies and rules so they are customer-friendly and training each employee to become a master at service recovery.

Too many executives think employees are born with good customer skills. They fail to realize that employees must be trained continuously in the basics of customer service. Look at Tiger Woods, the most successful golfer on earth. That success is not due to his

If you want your employees to provide service so awesome that is wows your customers, the fundamentals must combine with flawless execution.

good looks or incredible smile, it's due to the fact that he spends more time than any other golfer on the circuit practicing the basics and fundamentals of the game. Sure, Tiger still loses a lot of matches, but he's an exceptional golfer because he has not only mastered the fundamentals of the game but continues to practice and perfect them.

It's the same with employees. They must be trained in customer service and follow up that training with continuous practice in order to master the skills that will result in a loyal following for your products and services. Professional athletes spend hours each week practicing the basics. When your favorite team loses, it's usually because they poorly executed the fundamentals. It is very difficult to master the basics and to have flawless execution, but for those athletes—and employees— who do so, the sky is the limit. They will emerge as winners.

If you want your employees to provide service so awesome that is wows your customers, the fundamentals must combine with flawless execution. I strongly recommend that all organizations spend 10 percent of their advertising and marketing budgets on training employees in the art of customer service, service recovery, and empowerment.

Advertising will bring a customer to you—once. The customer experience is what will bring him back to you. Advertising is aimed at the masses; customer service is aimed at the individual.

Every employee must be trained to be knowledgeable about your products and services and to retain your customers by providing the best service possible. Unfortunately, many companies feel that, if they spend $25,000 to $200,000 on the design of a customer-service training program, they must use it for the next five to 10 years. Dell, which spend millions of dollars every month in creating and running new advertising,

Advertising is aimed at the masses; customer service is aimed at the individual.

knows the importance of developing fresh ads to keep the buying public interested in its products. They wouldn't think of running the same commercial for five or 10 years, or even for five months.

The money it spends on advertising, combined with the exceptional service it provides, has made Dell the number one computer systems company in the world. Its sales as of January 31, 2005, were $49.2 billion, a 19 percent increase over the previous year. Its profits also increased by 20 percent, to $4.3 billion.

Industry surveys consistently rank Dell number one in service and customer satisfaction. The company has mastered e-service. It has speed, apparent in the fact that its computers are made to order and shipped within four hours. The company effectively uses technology, not only in its computers but in its entire marketing plan.

Price also is critical to Dell's success. The company is brutal in eliminating costs, and it passes those savings on to its

Everything at Dell is built around service.

Ideally, you want to launch a new training program at least every six months.

customers with some of the lowest prices in the world. Everything at Dell is built around service. That's why it is a service leader –and an incredibly successful one.

Ideally, you should spend 40 hours a year training and developing your workforce to deliver superior customers service. You should introduce a new training program at least every six months in order to have a major impact on employees. You can't graduate from college by showing up for just one class. Customer service training is a process that is needed in order to change behaviors and attitudes, that teaches and reinforces the skills necessary to provide superior service.

You can go to any educational institution in any corner of the world and find that the fundamentals of customer service are never taught there. Too many companies believe that an hour or two of training is all that is necessary for their employees to become skilled in customer service.

General Electric is so focused on the skills of its employees that the company terminates 10 percent of its workers each year. That 10 percent represents the lowest-performing members of General Electric's workforce.

When employees don't respond to your efforts to train them in the art of customer service, help them find a job with your favorite competitor.

Ideally, you want to launch a new training program every six months-- and make sure it is interactive and includes lots of role playing. If you want employees to be able to master service recovery, provide several hours of training and focus much of that time on role playing.

All professional sports teams spend hours each week practicing the basics, the fundamentals, in preparation for their next game. When they lose, it's because they didn't flawlessly execute the basics. Thousands of Olympians practice their skills eight hours a day, seven days a week, for four years in

When employees don't respond to the art of service, help them find a job with your favorite com-petitor.

Why are organizations so reluctant to train and develop a high-performing, customer-driven work force?

preparation for what often is a 60-second event. The gold medal winner usually wins by a fraction of a second or a point.

Why are organizations so reluctant to train and develop a high-performing, customer-driven workforce? Some fear that, if they spend money training a more productive staff, those employees will move on and take jobs with other companies. What is worse, however, is not to train those employees and have them stay with you.

Employees also should invest in themselves if they want to get promoted and make more money. They shouldn't wait for the company to invest in them. If they want to be on a fast track and further their careers, they need to spend money every month to build themselves from within. They need to read a book on self-improvement every month.

The safest investment employees will ever make is in themselves. Anything they can do to improve their self-image, self-confidence, self-worth, leadership skills, and technical skills will make them more valuable. Employees should take advantage of every seminar and training program they can get the company to fund. And, they should always thank their employers for investing in them. A thank-you letter goes a long way.

Unfortunately, many employees don't want to take advantage of training opportunities, often using the excuse that they're too busy to do so. A sharp chain saw or axe cuts more trees in less time than a dull one. In my book, *Ca$hing In*, I explain that the only thing that prevents an employee from getting ahead is that employee and his or her self-imposed limitations. I strongly recommend that employees volunteer to attend seminars on weekends and evenings. If they read one self-improvement book a month for 10 years, they will have read 120 books, been promoted, and surely will be making more money. They must invest in their minds, not just in their appearances and their portfolios.

Employees must invest in their minds, not just in their appearances and their portfolios.

DON'T make excuses or lie to cover up a mistake.

DON'T point out a customer's misunderstanding.

DON'T pass the blame off or speak disparagingly about another employee or the organization.

- Take responsibility.
- Sincerely apologize.
- Don't place blame.
- Thank the customer for pointing out the problem.

42 NOTES

6

Empow-
erment

Empowerment is the backbone of service recovery. It's impossible to be a service leader, to be customer centric and focus on a service strategy without empowerment. Webster defines empower as: to give power, authority to; authorize; to enable, permit; to give ability to.

My definition of empowerment is to give employees the authority to do whatever it takes, on the spot, to take care of a customer to that customer's satisfaction—not to the organization's satisfaction. I have never had a CEO from anywhere in the world disagree with that definition. They know the cost of a defecting customer.

Service Recovery requires empowerment at all levels.

They realize the cost, in both time and money, involved when a customer complaint rises through the ranks and lands on the CEO's desk. Had an employee used common sense and focused on resolving the issue to the customer's satisfaction, the situation would have been handled with the customer's first contact with an employee.

Most executives believe their employees are empowered. And most employees would agree, as long as they follow the policies and procedures set forth by the company. What that means is that there really is **no** empowerment.

Service recovery requires empowerment at all levels. It requires a commitment by everyone in the organization to take whatever steps are necessary to ensure customer satisfaction. Effective empowerment means employees can bend and break the rules, can do whatever they have to do to have an overly happy customer.

Most policies and procedures are inflexible. They do not meet the different needs and demands of individual customers.

The main reason most employees do not make empowered decisions is that they fear they will be fired. Their perception is that it's easier to replace a customer than it would be to find another job. And yet I suspect very few employees have been fired for making an empowered decision and having overly happy customers.

Rarely will you find empowered employees at the front line. Yet, if you ask to speak to a manager, that manager often will be able to make the decision to help you. Most customers, however, are not overly assertive. They won't ask to speak to a manager and give the company one more chance to solve their problem. They just give up, leave, and don't come back.

Rarely will you find empowered employees at the front line.

In the meantime, organizations will spend a fortune on advertising to bring in new customers. Service role models, however, understand the power of empowerment in attracting and keeping customers.

Empowerment only works if it happens on the front line, with the employee who is paid the least but has 99 percent of the contact with your customers. Look at your own organization. Are employees reprimanded when they make a decision to satisfy the customer?

Look at your own organization. Are employees reprimanded when they make a decision to satisfy customers?

Let's look at credit card companies as an example. If you have ever been late making a payment and call to have the late fee waived for what you feel is a legitimate reason, often the employee on the other end of the line will refuse to do so. But, if you ask to speak to the manager and explain the situation, 90 percent of the time that late fee will be waived.

Credit card companies make a fortune on interest. And most of us receive one or more credit card offers a week. How loyal are you to your credit card firm?

The employee who does not make an empowered decision should be fired.

What sets one such firm apart from another? Would you jump ship, or are you loyal to your credit card company because it is a service leader and does whatever is necessary to ensure that you are a satisfied customer?

More than 40 percent of credit card holders make the minimum payment each month. Many people live from paycheck to paycheck, so waiving a $25 late fee can be a big deal for them. However, many executives and employees feel that waiving that fee will result in the company going broke, policies being violated, and employees being fired.

In reality, the employee who does not make an empowered decision that will result in a satisfied customer is the one who should be fired. That is the signal service leaders should send to employees throughout the company.

Most organizations talk about empowerment and truly think they practice it, yet their employees have never been trained to provide it. And most managers and supervisors have not been trained on how to reinforce empowerment or how to confront employees who have not practiced it.

Most employees prefer the safety of rules and policies. It's much easier for them to say, "I'm sorry, sir, but that is our policy."

Consider the expense of empowerment as part of your marketing and advertising budget.

But, it's much more effective to say, "Sir, of course. I appreciate you bringing this to our attention. No one is more important to our company than you. I would be delighted to take care of this for you."

Let's go back to the example of the credit card company. If you took that $25 late fee—the one you refused to waive—and went to your advertising company and said you wanted to use that $25 to attract a new customer to replace the one you just lost, what kind of response do you think you'd get?

Consider the expense of empowerment as part of your marketing and

Price alone is not a competitive weapon.

advertising budget. I have flown on Virgin Blue in Australia several times. The airline's employees are young and attractive, and the prices are extremely low. But owner Richard Branson has never trained those employees to be empowered. They are empowered only to follow the airline's policies. They are not in the same league as employees at JetBlue in the United States, which is focused on customer service and believes in and supports empowerment.

Price alone is not a competitive weapon. Southwest Airlines and JetBlue in the United States understand the service strategy and have empowered their employees to provide the best possible service to their customers. Virgin Blue copies the pricing formula of those two airlines but has neglected the service strategy.

Jason Ward, director of Customer Commitment for JetBlue says, "Loyalty at JetBlue means customers might not always like what you do, but they'll keep coming back based on the fact that they know you will be honest with them and take care of them. I don't care what business you're in, the purpose of that business is to have happy, paying customers who repeat and refer."

Is the customer always right? No, Ward says, but "it doesn't matter. What matters is how do you respond to and solve the customers' probems? Their problems are your problems."

At JetBlue, employees are directed to base all decisions on safety, integrity, caring, passion, and fun. "These values should be our values," Ward says. "There is a place for policies and procedures, but not in customer-helping areas. We teach our people to start with a 'yes' and to use their brains. Policies and procedures start with a 'no' and therefore shut the brain off."

The folks at JetBlue go above and beyond the call of duty to take care of their customers. That includes being proactive, which means they e-mail check-in reminders to customers taking red-eye flights because, Ward says, it can

"We teach our people to start with a 'yes' and to use their brains," says Jason Ward at JetBlue.

If you don't have empowered employees you will never have Service Recovery.

be confusing to a customer if their flight departs at 12:15 a.m. and check-in is actually at 11:15p.m. the night before. "If we have a delay or an irregular operation, it is our goal to send e-mails to customers advising them of the reason for the delay, how we are compensating for the issue, and to offer an apology,"

At JetBlue, service recovery is a way of life.

If you don't have empowered employees you will never have service recovery. Employees must make fast decisions and spend the company's money to move a customer from hell to heaven in 60 seconds or less. Empowerment must be reinforced. Employees who do not make empowered decisions must be reprimanded. In fact, I suggest that you fire employees who refuse to use empowerment. They will cost you too much. They will drive your customers away and leave you having to spend millions of dollars in an attempt to attract new customers and keep your company afloat.

Empowerment is essential to the
success of service recovery. It:

- Tells customers that you will put them first.

- Allows transactions to function smoothly.

- Builds and strengthens customer relationships.

- Saves money.

- Creates an amiable work environment.

7

Kiss Restrictive Policies Goodbye

Whⁿ a customer approaches an
employee and asks for help with a
problem, most often the employee's
response is, "We have a policy." Rather
than helping the customer, those words
are like pouring gasoline on a fire. They
make the situation more explosive and
increase the chances of losing that
customer.

While a company's policies and
procedures can leave customers
frustrated and angry, employees see
them as security blankets that protect
them from having to make decisions,
which often involve taking risks. Policies
and procedures and strict systems
provide a safety net for those employees.
If they had to make decisions when faced

To customers, employees are the company.

with a customer complaint, they risk being reprimanded or possibly fired.

Many top executives also prefer strict policies because they don't trust their customers or their employees. Without strict policies, they believe customers will take advantage of the company by intimidating employees who then will give away the store just to get an angry customer out of their face. Executives, for the most part, realize that their front-line employees are the least paid and least trained people in the organization and don't trust them to make good decisions.

What they should realize is that those front-line employees also are the people who have daily, face-to-face contact with customers. To customers, those employees are the company. They must do more than take the customer's money in exchange for products or services. They must service that customer. That means answering questions about those products and services in an effort to help the customer make an informed buying decision. It also means delivering those products and services in a timely manner. And, finally, it means resolving complaints when the customer has a problem with the company.

Bureaucrats love policies and procedures because they eliminate the need to think, to make decisions. The larger the organization, the more it focuses on policies and procedures. What those bureaucrats fail to realize is that replacing a customer who is on the receiving end of a ridiculous policy that prevents him from being satisfied with your service is much more expensive that providing the type of service that would keep him from defecting.

And yet an organization's policies and procedures prevent employees from doing their jobs well and providing the type of service that will keep customers coming back to do business with the company. Too many executives think that customer service means doing

The larger the organization, the more it focuses on policies and procedures.

whatever is necessary to satisfy the customer—as long as the actions taken fall in line with corporate policies and procedures. While that might work for the company, at least in the short run, it does not work for the customer, who will quickly defect and head to the competition.

For example, when you clear Customs and Immigration while flying with Delta Airlines in Atlanta, Georgia, you are required to stand in line to re-check your luggage. It takes up to an hour and costs millions of dollars a month in extra labor costs. Many passengers also miss their connecting flights, which further increases costs and customer dissatisfaction. Other airlines simply have agents who take your luggage while you walk to your connecting flight, which reduces the time to just a few minutes.

Here's another example: In Nigeria, five-star hotels are not used to customers paying by credit card, so it takes 40 minutes to check in and 20 minutes to check out. Those hotels should set up an

Eliminate dumb policies, rules and procedures.

The hours that most businesses are open often are designed to please management, not customers.

electronic credit card process at the front desk and empower their employees to process credit card payments.

On the other hand, most banks never open before their scheduled "bankers' hours." Commerce Bank, however, opens 10 minutes before it is scheduled to do so, which avoids long lines for customers and results in customers who are overly happy. It also stays open 10 minutes later than its scheduled closing time. The hours that most businesses are open often are designed to please management, not customers. I recommend that you consider opening earlier and staying open later. Commerce Bank's hours are 7:30 a.m. to 8 p.m. weekdays, 8 a.m. to 6 p.m. Saturdays, and 11 a.m. to 4 p.m. Sundays.

If you want to be a service leader and retain your customers, you must take two steps:

1. Eliminate dumb policies, rules, and procedures. You can have the most customer-focused employees in the

world, but if you have policies in place that prevent them from effectively serving the customer, you will destroy the customer relationship.

2.   Create specific procedures around service recovery that force employees to spend your money to keep customers by effectively handling their complaints and taking them from hell to heaven in 60 seconds or less and creating a loyal customer base that will be the envy of your competitors.

Create specific procedures around Service Recovery that force employees to spend your money.

If you encourage, even force, your employees to use service recovery, you will cultivate a loyal customer following, customers who are loyal for life. And it won't cost you a lot. For example, if you head a car rental company, you could satisfy a complaining customer by offering her a free upgrade or a coupon for a one-day free car rental. Instituting a policy that would require your employees to give the customer

Commerce Bank is the most customer-driven bank in the world and a great role model for any organization.

something of value would cost you virtually nothing out of pocket but has the potential of transforming an angry customer into a happy one who will continue to do business with you.

Commerce Bank in Philadelphia, New York and New Jersey is the most customer-driven bank in the world and a great role model for any organization. One of the reasons it is a $31-billion bank and has a 10-year, 29 percent annual return compared to the 18 percent return that Wal-Mart and 16 percent return Home Depot have is that it pays $50 to any employee who identifies a stupid policy or rule that should be eliminated or revised. With more than 11,000 employees, it's important for Commerce to have each of them looking for ways for the organization to become more customer-driven.

Look at your own organization's policies. Can an employee be fired or reprimanded for enforcing your policies? The problem is that your customers can—and will—fire your company every day for not meeting their expectations when it comes to customer service. And, once they fire you, they will tell everyone they know about your poor service. In doing so they will jeopardize your marketing and advertising campaigns.

The solution is to train employees at all levels of your organization to understand that their only goal should be to take care of your customers, to become customer-centric and focus on having overly happy customers. Service recovery is the magic you must use when you make a mistake. Your policy should be, "Yes, sir, we would be happy to help you out. No one is more important to us than you."

As I present my strategic customer service seminars throughout the world to all levels of management, I have discovered that very few executives understand service recovery. When asked to share service recovery examples, few can do so. And yet, it is service recovery that can drive their business and determine the success of their organizations.

Service Recovery is the magic you must use when you make a mistake.

Give free products or services.

Consider adopting service recovery policies that are enforced with specific free products or services so employees don't have to think about what to give disgruntled customers as a way of apologizing for the situation and to get them to return. Some companies pre-print coupons with discounts already established.

> After you have identified a customer problem, taken responsibility for the mistake and make an empowered decision. The final and most critical step is to give the customer something of value.
>
> Customers spread the word and remain loyal when you give them something for their trouble and let them know that they are valued.

> Every organization has something of value it can give to a customer who has experienced a problem.
>
> *What does your organization manufacture, sell, or provide as a service that costs less than the value it has in the eyes of your customers?*

8 | Moving Heaven and Earth

Service recovery means moving heaven and earth to satisfy the customer. It is not an easy concept for many companies to grasp—or to implement. Managers and supervisors have not been trained to reinforce the concept of service recovery. Employees have not been trained, inspired, coached, or motivated to provide it.

In developing countries, frontline employees make on average between $50 and $400 a month. In developed countries those figures are between $1,000 and $2,000 a month. Many executives and managers are uncomfortable with the thought of someone in China, who makes $50 a month, having the authority to move heaven and earth to satisfy a customer.

Ritz Carleton employees are empowered to spend up to $2,000 to solve a customer's problems.

On the other hand, service leaders like those at the Ritz Carlton expect their employees to do so. Ritz Carlton employees are expected to please customers and to solve their problems. Each new employee at the Ritz Carlton receives 130 hours of training and is recertified on an annual basis. They also are empowered. In fact, employees who are made aware of a customer complaint are empowered to spend up to $2,000 to solve that customer's problem.

While on a business trip in Sydney, Australia, I discovered I had no local currency, only $100 U.S. bills. It was a Sunday morning and no currency exchange businesses were open. I didn't even have money for a cup of coffee. I left my rental apartment and drove by a Four Seasons Hotel. I parked the car and went into the lobby. At the front desk, I asked if they could exchange U.S. currency for me. The employee said she could and asked for my room number. When I told her I was not a guest at the hotel, she said the hotel's policy was that she could make currency exchanges for hotel guests only.

I asked the woman if she were empowered. "No," she replied. I then pushed a little harder and said that I thought the Four Seasons had an empowered workforce. After trying several approaches to the situation, I asked to speak with the managing director. At that point, the employee responded, "I will make an exception this time and make the exchange for you." I would suspect that the management at the Four Seasons would have been disappointed with this employee, because it wants an empowered, customer-driven workforce that will attract and retain customers.

One of the reasons executives and employees don't understand why it is critical to move heaven and earth to satisfy a customer is that they don't understand the lifetime value of that

Most executives don't understand the lifetime value of a customer.

customer. They have no idea what their customer defection rates are and have no grasp of the cost of a defecting customer. Most firms look at the immediate value of a transaction. They don't appreciate how much money can disappear with a defecting customer. They don't realize that the fate of that customer—and of the company—is in their hands.

Employees throughout the world rarely are trained in customer service.

Employees throughout the world rarely are trained in customer service. Rather, they are instructed to follow the policies and procedures that bureaucrats love to create. It's not fair to expect employees to move heaven and earth to satisfy a customer when they have never been trained to do so, receive little recognition for their work, don't feel valued or appreciated, and have been reprimanded in the past for not following the company's policies and procedures.

Another roadblock to service recovery is that it forces employees to admit that they or the organization they work for made a mistake. For many employees,

Moving heaven and earth is a mindset that is more powerful than any advertising.

losing face and having to admit to a mistake is more than they can handle. I challenge you to count the times you have had an employee say, "I made a mistake. It's my fault. Let me take care of this for you."

Moving heaven and earth is a mindset that is more powerful than any advertising. It's built around empowerment. When problems arise, you want employees who have only one goal: to have an overly happy customer. When employees accomplish that goal, celebrate the event. Publicize it in the company newsletter or magazine. Make sure that management at every level of the organization celebrates that employee and his or her service recovery efforts.

If you train your employees to move heaven and earth to satisfy your customers, you will have a base of loyal customers on which to grow your business.

Don't be cheap. If you must spend money to keep a customer from defecting, then you must.

9

Is the Customer Always Right?

Many executives and employees feel the customer is lying, trying to rip off the company, trying to get something for nothing. I suspect that 1 to 3 percent of the time this is indeed the case.

To avoid getting ripped off by those customers, however, many organizations implement policies that punish the other 97 to 99 percent who have legitimate complaints and requests. In other words, even if the customer isn't always right, you must treat him as if he is.

Let me give you a personal example. I brought in the measurements for a new window and frame for my home to The Home Depot. When the window and frame arrived, I had $70-an-hour

His attitude and concern over my situation made this a rewarding experience.

installers come in to install them. Unfortunately, I had it measured incorrectly, and the window wouldn't fit. The installers brought it back to The Home Depot—charging me $200 for their time. They said they felt The Home Depot should have caught the measurement error.

I ordered a replacement window that was $150 less than the one I had originally ordered. I had paid cash for that order but the store gave me an in-store credit for the difference in price. The assistant manager said the store's computer would not let him give me cash back, but he offered to sell me the new window at cost. I agreed, and he then gave me $135 back in cash.

He also said, "I wish you had called us right away, because we would have sent someone over to pick up the original window." His attitude and concern over my situation made this a rewarding experience. It was service recovery at its best. I spend thousands of dollars at The Home Depot every year—and this is why.

The Home Depot's focus on customer service is the reason it earned $5 billion on $73 billion in sales in 2004. That is why The Home Depot has 1,700 stores and is the second largest retailer in the United States. It's not surprising that a recent study ranked The Home Depot's associates 40 percent higher than the competition in customer service and product knowledge.

Bernie Marcus, co-founder of The Home Depot wrote the following in his book *Built From Scratch*: "Customer cultivation is just like cultivating a tomato plant. Prepare the soil; maybe put some additives in it. Plant the seed. Water it. Prune it. Fertilize it. Apply insecticides. It will always grow bigger if you cultivate it. If you cultivate it, it will bear more fruit."

"Customer cultivation is just like cultivating a tomato plant," Bernie **Marcus wrote in his book** *Built From Scratch*.

I'm also impressed with comments Bob Nardelli, CEO of The Home Depot made. He said, "The biggest threat to success is complacency. The biggest competitor we have is not Lowe's [the number two home-improvement retailer]; it's us."

Another fine example of a service-driven organization is Costco. The company is the sixth largest retailer in the United States, the ninth largest in the world, and was ranked number 29 on the 2004 Fortune 500 list. Costco has 449 stores throughout the world and had sales of $47.1 billion during 2004, a 13 percent increase over 2003 sales. Profits in 2004 were an impressive $882 million.

What accounts for those impressive numbers? Service. Customers can return anything at anytime. Costco has the highest customer satisfaction ratio of any top specialty retailer in the United States, according to a study conducted by the University of Michigan. That's apparent when you compare Costco with Sam's Club, which is owned by Wal-Mart. Sam's Club has 71 percent more stores in the

At Costco, customers can return anything at anytime.

You must trust your customers and treat them as if they're always right.

United States, but Costco's total sales are 5 percent higher. Costco is one of very few retailers in the world that understands and has mastered the service strategy more effectively than Wal-Mart.

One of the biggest obstacles to implementing service recovery is the perception that the customer is lying or trying to rip off the company. This rarely happens. The cost of attempting to prevent 1 to 3 percent of dishonest customers from trying to rip you off is expensive and will cause you to lose millions of dollars worth of positive word-of-mouth advertising that results from service recovery.

Costco is a perfect example of a company that trusts its customers. You must trust your customers and treat them as if they're always right.

It's difficult, if not impossible, for an employee or even a manager to identify those customers who want to take advantage of your organization. Perception is reality. You might feel a customer is wrong or is lying, but you can never convey that. You cannot communicate how you really feel about the situation.

You must trust your customers. You must solve their problems and give them something of value that will keep them coming back to you. Even if some of those customers are taking advantage of you, they will help spread the word about your wonderful customer service, which will bring in more customers, and increase your revenues and profits.

So, is the customer always right? No, but you must treat him or her as if he or she is.

> **Is the customer always right? No, but you must treat him or her as if he or she is.**

> Policies and procedures can become a security blanket that protects the untrained employee from taking risks in practicing service recovery.

> When policies and procedures leave customers frustrated and angry, they defeat the purpose of service recovery.

10 Service Recovery Examples

Giving a dissatisfied customer something of value is an effective method of getting that customer to return to you time and time again and to sing your praises to anyone within earshot. What do you have to give customers that would be of minimal cost to you but would be of value to your customers?

Following are some examples that will help you better understand the opportunity you have to let those customers know that you value them and their business and to make them loyal for life.

What is the real cost? Next to nothing.

Hotels

You can upgrade your guest to a suite. Or give her a free two-night stay, or a complimentary meal. I was unhappy with the Point Hilton Tapatio Cliffs Resort in Phoenix, Arizona. Simply put, the service was nowhere near what it had been during previous stays. In response to my complaint, the hotel sent me a letter inviting my wife and me to return and spend two nights as guests of the hotel. When we arrived, they upgraded our room to a suite.

What was the real cost to the hotel? Next to nothing. What did the hotel receive in return for its service recovery efforts? My wife and I spent $197 on meals and tennis. The hotel also kept us as customers and can count on our repeat business.

Another example of a hotel that has implemented service recovery is the Ritz Carlton in Kansas City. I complained about the problems I had encountered in getting from the airport to the hotel. In response to my complaint, the hotel upgraded my room to the presidential suite. What was the hotel's out-of-pocket cost for doing so? Nothing. (My only complaint after the upgrade was that my wife was not with me to enjoy the luxury.)

Restaurants

When a customer complains that she made a reservation for dinner at 7 p.m. but wasn't seated until 7:45 p.m., there are several steps you can take to turn her dissatisfaction into satisfaction. Give her and her guests a free round of drinks or free appetizers or a coupon for a free dinner in the future. The real cost to the restaurant might be $2 while the value in the customer's eyes is $16 to $20. The first two options will appease her that evening; the third option will get her to return.

Even fast-food businesses can give customers something of value that will

Give customers something of value that will get them to return.

What was the real cost to McDonalds for those chicken McNuggets?

get them to return. I recently ordered chicken McNuggets from a drive-through at a McDonald's. When I reached my office and opened the bag, I realized the employee had failed to include sweet and sour sauce. I called the restaurant and talked to the store manager, who said he would put my name on a list for free chicken McNuggets the next time I came in.

I returned to that McDonald's about six weeks later, but the employee at the drive-thru who took my order would not give me the free McNuggets. We had a rather lengthy conversation, while the people in the cars waiting behind me began to honk their horns in frustration. A supervisor finally came to the window and voided the charge for my order. She did it not because I had been promised a free order but because of all the horns honking behind me. I haven't been back to that McDonald's since.

What was the real cost to McDonald's for those chicken McNuggets? Probably 50 cents. But it lost me as a customer because of its poor service recovery.

Employees must be trained to apologize for mistakes, take responsibility for them, and practice Service Recovery.

McDonald's consistently has the lowest customer satisfaction ratings of any fast-food firm in the United States, according to annual surveys conducted by the University of Michigan.

When a fast-food restaurant takes longer than is acceptable to get your meal, it could easily throw in a free order of French fries or a free soft drink. The cost to the restaurant might be only 20 cents but the return on that investment could easily be 100 times that amount. The magic in service recovery comes from empowered employees who understand that their single purpose is to take care of customers and to ensure that they are satisfied and will return.

Employees must be trained to apologize for mistakes, take responsibility for them, and practice service recovery. A restaurant employee should say, "Ma'am, we made a mistake. Your order was misplaced. While we process it, please let me get you a free round of drinks or offer you a complimentary dessert."

That is powerful. That customer will talk positively about your restaurant during the rest of the meal and probably will tell many of her friends about you. And all it cost you was $2. That's not a bad return on your investment.

What do you have of value that you can give away free?

Airlines

Airlines on occasion are faced with angry passengers because a flight is delayed. They can offer those passengers a free drink at a cost to the airline of an estimated 50 cents per passenger but has a retail value in the eyes of those passengers of $5 or $6 each. An airline that makes a mistake in a passenger's reservation could upgrade that passenger to first class at no real cost to the company.

Most airlines have frequent flyer programs. While on a Northwest/KLM flight from Amsterdam to Minneapolis, Minnesota, the airline had a fuel problem and had to stop and refuel in Newfoundland. As an apology, the

A formal service recovery policy is critical to a service strategy.

airline gave each passenger a pre-printed coupon book that included a coupon good for $50 off the next flight of $200 or more, an MCI 10-minute free phone card for calls within the United States, 2,000 free World Perks bonus miles, and a coupon good toward $10 in meals and beverages at the airport or in-flight liquor beverages. The airline had a formal service recovery policy in place, which is critical to a service strategy.

That was great service recovery.

Dry Cleaners

I wear custom-made shirts. I took them to a new one-hour Martinizing Dry Cleaner. When I picked up those shirts and got home, I noticed one of them was torn to shreds. The employee hadn't mentioned it while I was there. When I returned, the employee argued about the price to replace that custom-made shirt. After repeated calls to the customer service manager, the dry cleaner finally paid me for the shirt it had ruined. It was too little too late, and I never went back.

What that dry cleaner should have done was put a note in with my shirts acknowledging and apologizing for the situation and then talked to me about it when I picked up my shirts and offered me $50 in free laundry and dry cleaning services. The out-of-pocket cost to the dry cleaner might have been $5, but it would have forced me to return as a customer.

Service recovery includes giving the customer something of value that will entice him to return to you and to purchase your product or service again.

Car Rental Companies

Car-rental companies have several options when it comes to service recovery. They can upgrade the customer to a larger car or give her a coupon for one or two free days on a future car rental.

Most companies don't understand the power of service recovery.

Cell Phone Companies

Telecommunications companies spend a fortune on advertising and phone giveaways to get new customers. That might get a customer, but it won't necessarily keep a customer. Most cell phone companies don't understand the power of service recovery.

They fail to implement a simple strategy that, for example, responds to a customer who has had trouble with her new cell phone by saying, "Mrs. Brown, I'm very sorry your new phone is not working properly. This is very embarrassing to us. Can you please return it to your local store for a free replacement? I also am waiving your first two months fee for the inconvenience we caused."

Or, if a customer is so dissatisfied with his service that he is contemplating changing carriers, a company representative might say, "Mr. Chen, I'm sorry to hear you are considering changing carriers because of the problems you have experienced with you cell phone. You are very important to our company. We can't afford to lose you. Let me give you a free replacement phone and 1,000 minutes of free air time."

In this example, it's a given that you are going to lose the customer. And, when that customer signs on with one of your competitors, that competitor will more than likely give him a free phone. Why not give the customer a free phone, throw in some free minutes, and keep the customer for yourself? The 1,000 minutes costs you virtually nothing but are significant enough to force the customer to continue to use your service. I use the word "force" because, emotionally and psychologically, people are reluctant to pass up anything of value that is significant and free.

Emotionally and psychologically, people are reluctant to pass up anything of value that is significant and free.

Software Firms

Let's say Mr. Martinez is unhappy with the new CRM software he purchased and calls you to complain. Here's one way to handle that call.

"I am so sorry you had this problem."

"Mr. Martinez, I am sorry to hear that your company is unhappy with the new CRM software you purchased from us. Let me get our technical person to help you, at no charge, and because of the inconvenience I am going to e-mail you a free software package upgrade that will help you better leverage the CRM software you just purchased. Again, I am so sorry you had this problem."

The cost to the software company is virtually nothing. On the other hand, if Mr. Martinez returns the software, the company will have to refund his money and will lose him and any potential business from him in the future.

Supermarkets

I have never had a supermarket not refund my money when a product I purchased did not live up to my expectations. Typically, even a receipt is not necessary to get a refund. A supermarket's biggest problem with service recovery is that many customers don't complain when they are unhappy; they simply don't return to the store.

If Ms. Schmidt purchased peaches from you and discovered within two days that they have spoiled, what are you going to do to keep her as a customer? Here's what I'd do. "Ms. Schmidt, I am sorry about this. Please let me replace the peaches and give you two more pounds at no charge. Your satisfaction is important to me. Without customers such as yourself we would not exist."

The cost of the extra two pounds of peaches might be $3, not much when you consider that supermarkets spend a fortune on advertising each week. Even if a supermarket gave 100 customers two pounds of peaches in a week, it's still a drop in the bucket, a small price to pay to retain those customers.

Supermarkets consistently offer the best service among all retail sectors. They know the lifetime value of a customer is

Many customers don't complain; they simply don't return.

Go above and beyond the call of service.

$50,000. So spending $3 to keep $50,000 in business is a no-brainer.

Home and Garden Stores

More and more home and garden stores are offering 12-month guarantees on their perennials. It's important that, when a customer returns a plant that didn't survive, you make it easy for him to do so.

"Mr. Romero, I'm sorry the perennial you purchased from us didn't survive the winter. Let me replace the plant. It's important that you are satisfied with the quality of our plants and our service."

A few years ago, I ran into an exemplary employee at The Home Depot, who went above and beyond the call of service to ensure that he retained my business. His name is Kevin Larsen. I had purchased Ortho crab grass killer from The Home Depot at which he works, and the product ruined my lawn. I spent another $300 in an attempt to repair it.

The following spring, I noticed that the Ortho product had a money-back guarantee, so I asked Larsen for that company's telephone number. He asked what The Home Depot could do to solve my problem, but I insisted it was Ortho's problem, not The Home Depot's. After several telephone calls to Ortho during the next two months, however, I was told I wasn't eligible for the guarantee, because I didn't have the receipt for the $10 purchase or the empty chemical container.

On my next visit to The Home Depot, I mentioned my experience to Larsen, who asked me how much I had spent to repair my lawn. I told him. Larsen disappeared for a few minutes, then returned and handed me $300 in cash. I was flabbergasted—and impressed.

The Home Depot has done something I preach to my clients throughout the world. It has empowered its employees to do whatever it takes to satisfy the customer. I was so impressed with Larsen and with The Home Depot that,

The Home Depot had done something I preach to my clients throughout the world.

The Home Depot has empowered its employees to do whatever it takes to satisfy the customer.

during the following year, I spent more than $10,000 there. Why would I shop anywhere else?

Car Dealerships

Let's say Ms. Baxter brought her car in a second time to have you repair a problem she thought had been fixed the first time she brought it to you. Now, most of us intensely dislike bringing our cars in for repairs. It takes time and often leaves us without transportation for a day or two. The process requires that we enlist the help of a family member or friend to drive us home from the dealership and then back to the dealership to pick up the car when it's ready. When the customer must return the car again because the repairs were not done correctly, it is a major inconvenience.

Here's how I would handle this situation. "Ms. Baxter, I cannot apologize enough for this inconvenience. We will make the necessary repairs as quickly as possible. In the meantime, let me get you a free loaner car so you have something to drive while we work on your car. I'd also like to give you a coupon for a free oil change."

Spend real money on Service Recovery.

Neither the free oil change nor the loaner car will cost the dealership any real out-of-pocket money. Both, however, will compensate Ms. Baxter for being inconvenienced and will keep her as a customer.

Banks

Banks throughout the world typically have the worst service. Few banking executives understand service recovery. Waiving overdraft fees and reversing charges seem to be difficult decisions for them to make. It's apparently easier for them to spend more money on advertising to get new customers than it is to keep the ones they have.

Banks might need to spend real money on service recovery. Their product is money, so it makes sense that that is what they have to use to compensate their dissatisfied customers. Let's say a

Clients are not all equal.

customer had a problem that involved a deposit being lost or deposited in the wrong account, which resulted in several overdraft fees.

We'd expect the bank to waive the overdraft fees and call the customer or send him a letter apologizing for the problem. But that is not enough. That customer's creditors don't care who made the mistake or why. All they know is that the check the customer wrote bounced.

If the bank deposited $25 in that customer's account, that would be nice. But I don't think it's enough. US Bank in Minneapolis, Minnesota, offers $5 to customers when it makes an error. That amount is insignificant and has no real impact. In this case, I would recommend that the bank deposit at least $100 as compensation for the error and the resulting problems.

Clients are not all equal. A valued business customer might need a much greater compensation in order to continue to do business with the bank. The bank should identify the cost of acquiring a new customer. If that cost is $50, it then should use $50 as compensation for each service recovery incident.

Banks should use their money with maximum, targeted marketing—and that is their current customers.

Internet Service Providers

It's easy for an Internet service provider to have technical problems. They also have problems when it comes to customer loyalty, because it's so easy to switch providers. In order to keep a current but dissatisfied customer, an Internet service provider must be prepared to waive the service fee for one or two months.

I recommend that you calculate the average life of a current customer. If it is two to four years and the monthly service fee is $20, that's $720 for three years. If you waive $20 or $40 to keep that customer, you still keep $680 to

Calculate the average life of a current customer.

Keeping a customer should be your highest priority.

$700 that would have disappeared when that customer took her business elsewhere.

Keeping a customer should be your highest priority. It is 10 times less expensive to keep a current customer than it is to attract a new one through advertising. Fund your customer service and service recovery strategies from your advertising budget. It's a much more efficient use of your money.

Health Care Providers

Customers visiting a clinic, doctor's office or health care provider routinely find themselves facing missed, mismanaged or rescheduled appointments, lost insurance information and long wait times.
In response to problems, complaints and extraordinary wait times, customers could be offered special access to the doctor or clinician by cellphone or personal pager. With a doctor, access and speed are critical and service recovery can mean providing that access. A physical therapist could offer a patient whose appointment was abruptly rescheduled, a free massage. Any health care provider should have the

authority to at least waive a customer's co-pay in an effort to salvage the situation and maintain customer loyalty. Health care providers rarely utilize the power of service recovery to keep their customers and patients from defecting, but a clinic or doctor's office is no different than any other organization and an irate customer will fire you just as quickly as they would leave their cell phone company.

Are your employees empowered to bend and break the rules to create happy customers who will be loyal for life?

Credit Card Companies

Credit card companies make their money on interest, late fees, and over-the-credit limit fees. It's no wonder that consumers receive several credit card applications in the mail every week. And it follows that those consumers have no great loyalty to their credit card companies. They'll jump at the chance to get a better deal.

Two of the major problems credit card companies face are customers who don't pay their bills and customers who defect. Research shows that people spend much more money when they use credit cards rather than cash.

As a result, it's easy to send a payment in late or to spend more than the credit card limit.

When one of your customers has a problem, what do you do? Are your employees empowered to bend and break the rules to create happy customers who will be loyal for life? Your service recovery strategy could include lowering interest rates, waiving late and over-credit-limit fees, or correcting information that customers need to improve their credit ratings.

When a customer defects, you lose all that interest income. The concern bureaucrats have is what happen if a customer thinks she can repeat this on a regular basis? So what? Are you better off with an overly happy customer who pays a lot of interest or in keeping a $25 late fee and losing that customer?

11 Develop Effective Policies and Proce- dures

Put in place at least five examples of service recovery with strict instructions to employees to meet or exceed them.

Make sure management models the behavior on all levels.

Have pre-printed coupons with free services your employees must hand out when service issues arise. This way you are forcing management and employees to implement service recovery initiatives. Employees no longer will have to think about what to do. Empowerment is enforced.

Confront and reprimand employees who do not use empowerment and service recovery.

Celebrate examples of empowerment and service recovery until it becomes a way of life. Then celebrate even more.

Identify the top 6 flash points or incidents where empowerment and service recovery are critical. Make sure your examples are very specific.

Flash Point	Service Recovery Example	Real Cost	Perceived Value

Flash Point	Service Recovery Example	Real Cost	Perceived Value

Questions to Answer

- What is your defection rate?_____
- How much do you spend to acquire a new customer?

  _____

- What is the purchasing lifespan of a loyal customer?_____

Each year a loyal customer spends more. How much does your average customer spend each year over their life?

_____

Year	Sales Revenue
1	
2	
3	
4	
5	
6	
7	
8	
9	
10	
Total Sales Revenue	$

Each year a loyal customer beomes more profitable. What is the profit each year over the life of a loyal customer?

Year	Profit
1	
2	
3	
4	
5	
6	
7	
8	
9	
10	
Total Sales Revenue	$
Total Profit	$
Total Combined	$

If the lifetime value of loyal customer is $_____ , the cost for service recovery is peanuts when you look at the real cost of loosing a customer.

Spend your marketing money to keep customers.

Bain & Company's research shows you could double the growth of your business if you cut your defection rate by half. If you cut the defection rate by 5 percent, you can have a profit swing of 25 to 100 percent.

Your staff needs to move quickly when a problem arises. Spend your marketing money to keep customers. Fund this approach out of your marketing and advertising budget. And be generous.

If the customer comes back, you have a second chance to prove you are good at service. If the customer doesn't come back, all your marketing money went down the drain.

If a customer is overly happy and service recovery is practiced, however, you will have a customer who is loyal for life. Maximize word-of-mouth advertising.

Identify products or services that force a customer to come back to you.

Look for products and services that have value in the eyes of the customer and that do not cost your organization a lot of out-of-pocket money. If you're a florist, sending flowers is a great example. If you own a manufacturing company, the flowers are a 100 percent out-of-pocket expense.

If you are a telecommunications company and calls were dropped and customers are upset, giving those customers 500 minutes of free airtime forces them to keep using you.

Think of products or services that force a customer to come back to you. If service was extraordinarily bad, however, there might be nothing you can do that would retain that customer. My sister had a free roundtrip ticket on Air Tran Airways that she never used. The value was between $200 and $300. Sometimes the problem is so severe that nothing will appease the customer.

An apology and taking responsibility are the first two steps. The frosting on the cake is service recovery.

Have everyone role play in handling service recovery issues. If you cannot skillfully do it in a classroom, there is little chance it will happen on the frontline.

The cost to keep a customer is less expensive if done immediately by a frontline employee. Very few customers complain. They merely defect. Kiss the customer goodbye if you don't handle the situation immediately.

Most employees are reluctant to apologize and take responsibility for mistakes. To do so, however, is the very foundation of service recovery. Employees must apologize for the mistake, regardless of who made it. They must take responsibility for it on behalf of the company. And they must do whatever it takes to correct that mistake and to ensure that the customer is satisfied and will return to do business with the company time and time again.

Most employees are reluctant to apologize and take responsibility for mistakes.

Don't be cheap.

Ideally, you want each area of the company to come up with five to 10 service recovery examples. Make sure they have value. Don't be cheap. Your goal is to keep a customer and, secondly, to make the customer overly happy.

- Identify and help eliminate dumb policies, rules, and procedures that can destroy customer loyalty.

- Use service recovery to create specific policies that force you to prioritize customers.

- Make sure you can take customers from hell to heaven in 60 seconds or less.

- You know your customers best.

- You know what they need.

- You know what they want.

12 Worksheet for your firm

In order to design service recovery policies for your organization, you need to teach employees the art of service so they move from the paradigm of "this is just a customer" to "this is our most important and valued customer."

I suggest that each firm have at least five service recovery examples in place and then mandate that they are used to identify problems, service recovery solutions, the real cost of the product or service, and the perceived cost by the customer.

Service Problem	Recovery Solution	Real Cost	Perceived Value

Service Problem	Recovery Solution	Real Cost	Perceived Value
Airline flight is delayed	Offer 1,000 miles	$2	$20
Restaurant lost your reservation and you had to wait 60 minutes	Buy everyone a round of drinks	$1.60	$20
The doctor kept you waiting for 30 minutes	Waive the exam fee	$15	$75
Supermarket's $3 donuts were stale	Replace the donuts and give the customer another dozen, free	$3	$8
Problems with final bill for house construction	Complete work within five days and offer to fix anything else necessary while there	$100	$400
Bank charged a late fee for credit card payment made on time	Waive the late fee and waive the interest for the month	$35	$65
Candy manufacturer sells a defective box of chocolates	Send two replacement boxes of chocolates	$6	$30
Car wash does not clean the car well	Give coupons for three free car washes	$4.50	$18

Here are some examples of real and perceived values:

Airline: "I am sorry your flight was delayed. I have added 2,000 miles to your frequent flyer account" or, "We would like to upgrade you to first class."
Value: $20 and $300

Car rental firm: "I am sorry about the problem with your reservation. Can I upgrade you to a larger car at no extra charge?" Value: $80

Restaurant: "I apologize for losing your reservation and making you wait until 7:30 to be seated. Can we buy you a round of drinks while you wait for your table?" Value: $28

Cinema: "I am sorry you were unhappy with the film. Here are four tickets to a movie of your choice."
Value: $32

Home construction: "We apologize for not properly installing your shower door. We will fix the situation this morning and make any other adjustments you want in your home at no charge." Value: $250

Computer repair store: "I apologize for the problem you had with your computer. I am going to extend your warranty by one year." Value: $100

Hotel: "I am sorry the shower in your bathroom is not working properly. We'd like to upgrade you to a suite at no extra charge." Value: $200

Ski resort: "We apologize for the malfunction of the ski lift, which left you stranded for an hour. We'd like to give you two free lift tickets." Value: $147.

Dry cleaner: "We are sorry your shirt was torn. Here is $50 in coupons for free dry cleaning services." Value: $50.

Health Care: "I am sorry the doctor was delayed. The co-pay is waived for today." Value: $25

If you have thoughts, comments, or ideas about this book, I'd love to hear from you. Feel free to write or call.

John Tschohl
Service Quality Institute
9201 East Bloomington Freeway
Minneapolis, Minnesota 55420-3497 USA
952-884-3311 fax 952-884-8901
email: quality@servicequality.com
web-site: www.customer-service.com

Service Quality Institute provides a variety of customer, service recovery and recognition training programs that cover the entire work force. If you are interested in learning more about Service Quality Institute's training programs or about John Tschohl's seminars and speeches, please contact Service Quality Institute at the above address.

ALSO BY JOHN TSCHOHL

ACHIEVING EXCELLENCE THROUGH CUSTOMER SERVICE
(Best Sellers Publishing, 2002, ISBN: 0-9636268-4-1)

E-SERVICE
(Best Sellers Publishing, 2001, ISBN: 0-9636268-6-8, $24.95)

CASHING IN
(Best Sellers Publishing, 1995, ISBN: 0-9636268-2-5, $14.95)

THE CUSTOMER IS BOSS
(Best Sellers Publishing, 1993, ISBN: 0-9636268-0-9, $19.95)

Service Recovery Ideas

Service Recovery Problems

Service Recovery Solutions

Empowerment Initiatives

Celebration Ideas for Employee's Who Use Service
Recovery and Empowerment